The Split History of the

BATTLE OF FORT SUMTER:

CONFEDERATE PERSPECTIVE

BY STEVEN OTFINOSKI

CONTENT CONSULTANT:
Donald C. Elder III, PhD
Professor of History
Eastern New Mexico University

COMPASS POINT BOOKS
a capstone imprint

About the Author

Steven Otfinoski has written more than 180 books for young readers. Three of his nonfiction books have been named Books for the Teen Age by the New York Public Library. Steve also enjoys teaching college English and creative writing. He lives in Connecticut with his wife.

Source Notes

Union Perspective:

Page 14, line 6: Abraham Lincoln. "First Inaugural Address of Abraham Lincoln." 4 March 1861. 27 Sept. 2017. Yale Law School. The Avalon Project. http://avalon.law.yale.edu/19th_century/lincoln1.asp

Page 16, line 11: Charles Ward. "Letters addressed to Hon. James Buchanan, President of the United States, January 10th and 16th, 1861." Salem, Mass: *Salem Gazette*. 1866, p. 7. 24 Oct. 2017. https://archive.org/details/lettersaddressed00ward

Page 17, line 20: "Important Correspondence Preceding the Bombardment." *The New York Times*. 13 April 1861. 13 Oct. 2017. http://www.nytimes.com/1861/04/13/news/important-correspondence-preceding-the-bombardment.html?mcubz=0

Page 18, line 7: Shelby Foote. *The Civil War: A Narrative, Vol. 1*. New York: Vintage Books, 1986, p. 49.

Page 19, line 6: Abner Doubleday. *Reminiscences of Forts Sumter and Moultrie in 1860–'61*. New York: Harper & Brothers, 1876, pp. 143–144.

Page 23, line 12: Ibid., p. 158.

Page 28, line 21: Georgeanna Woolsey Bacon and Eliza Woolsey Howland. *Letters of a Family During the Civil War*. New Haven, Conn.: Tuttle, Morehouse & Taylor, 1899, p. 67.

Page 28, line 22: Ibid., p. 67.

Page 29, line 18: Derek Smith. *Sumter After the First Shots: The Untold Story of America's Most Famous Fort Until the End of the Civil War*. Mechanicsburg, Pa.: Stackpole Books, 2015, p. 314.

Confederate Perspective:

Page 5, line 5: Beth G. Crabtree and James W. Patton, eds. *Journal of a Secesh Lady: The Diary of Catherine Ann Devereux Edmondston*. Raleigh, N.C.: North Carolina Office of Archives and History, 1860–1866. p. 32.

Page 13, line 1: *The Civil War: A Narrative, Vol. 1*, p. 46.

Page 14, line 22: Francis Butler Simkins and Robert Hilliard Woody. *South Carolina During Reconstruction*. Chapel Hill: The University of North Carolina Press, 1932, p. 38.

Page 15, line 3: *The Civil War: A Narrative, Vol. 1*, p. 47.

Page 16, line 2: Ibid., p. 48.

Page 16, line 12: Ibid., p. 48.

Page 18, line 4: Ibid., p. 49.

Page 20, line 7: Mary Boykin Miller Chesnut. *A Diary from Dixie*. New York: D. Appleton and Company, 1905, p. 38.

Page 24, line 1: Ibid., p. 39.

Page 25, line 4: William Howard Russell. *My Diary North and South*. New York: Harper & Brothers, 1863, pp. 98–99.

Page 27, line 5: Henry Woodhead, ed. *Charleston: Voices of the Civil War*. Alexandria, Va.: Time-Life Books, 1997, p. 10.

Page 28, Line 2: Ibid., p. 157.

Table of Contents

SHARED RESOURCES

CHAPTER 1 SECESSION!

On the morning of January 9, 1861, the people of Charleston, South Carolina, awoke to the sound of cannon fire. Those closest to the harbor were stunned to see a ship churning up the channel toward federally held Fort Sumter, a U.S. flag flying from it.

The booming guns on nearby Morris Island were firing on the ship. It was attempting to bring supplies and possibly reinforcements to Fort Sumter, something South Carolina's troops would not allow. A month prior, such a scene might not have taken place. But South Carolina had seceded from the Union on December 20, 1860. The ship and the soldiers who occupied Fort Sumter were now the enemy.

Although cannons were visible at Fort Sumter's portholes, they remained strangely silent. Suddenly the supply ship, still under fire, turned and retreated down the channel. Charleston's citizens felt a mixture of relief and anger. As eyewitness Catherine Edmondston wrote in her diary: "Eleven guns in all were fired. Good God! Is this true? Is this the beginning of the Civil War, of which we have heard so much . . .?"

It was not the start of the Civil War, just another fateful step that drew the nation closer to it. It was not surprising that South Carolina was the first southern state to secede from the Union. The state had long been at odds with the federal government. For many years, South Carolina's economy relied on trade with European countries that bought its cotton and other products. For this reason, the state opposed new federal taxes on exported and imported goods that were passed in 1819, 1828, and 1832. The last tax made South Carolinians so angry that the state passed a law declaring the 1819 and 1828 taxes "null and void" in the state. President Andrew Jackson was so upset by this that he threatened to send federal soldiers to South Carolina to enforce the taxes. But when a revised tax bill was passed as a compromise the following year, South Carolina repealed the law.

Slavery was another issue where South Carolina felt its states' rights were in jeopardy. Slavery thrived in the South. There, farmers and owners of large plantations had relied on the unpaid labor of enslaved Africans for decades. But many people in the

Slavery was an important factor in the South's economy.
Many Southern plantations relied heavily on slave labor.

North were against slavery. Efforts by northern politicians to ban slavery in new territories so angered South Carolina that in 1850 the state threatened to secede from the Union. It did not secede then, partly because no other southern states would join it. Yet by 1860 the struggle between states' rights and the federal government's power had reached a boiling point in the South. The election of Republican Abraham Lincoln in November convinced South Carolinians that their rights, especially the right to own slaves, were at risk.

The Crittenden Compromise of 1860

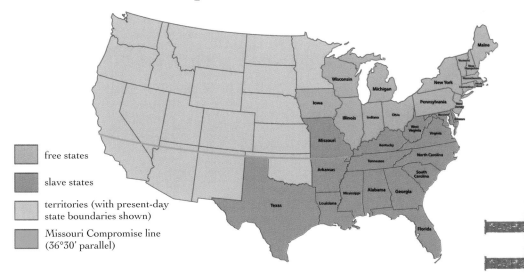

free states

slave states

territories (with present-day state boundaries shown)

Missouri Compromise line (36°30' parallel)

SEEKING A COMPROMISE

Some southerners looked desperately for a compromise that would prevent secession. In 1860 Senator John J. Crittenden of Kentucky proposed an amendment to the Constitution that would forbid Congress from ever abolishing slavery in the South. Another amendment would extend a line, first proposed in the Missouri Compromise 40 years earlier, across the United States to the Pacific coast. All states and territories north of the line would remain permanently free of slavery. Slavery would be legal in all territories south of the line. Newly elected President Lincoln was willing to allow slavery to continue in the South, but he did not want to legalize slavery in all territories south of the proposed line. He feared that if the second part of the Crittenden Compromise became law, the South might try to acquire even more lands farther south in Mexico and Central America and make them slave states as well.

Two days later, on December 20, South Carolina's lawmakers voted 169–0 to secede from the Union. On December 24, the U.S. House of Representatives received a letter written by four of South Carolina's representatives formally declaring secession.

South Carolina was officially a separate, independent state, but it still had a federal garrison operating at Fort Moultrie on Sullivan's Island in Charleston Harbor. The sight of the American flag flying over the fort was seen as an insult by many of Charleston's residents. Earlier, before formal secession, a mob had threatened to attack the fort. But one of Charleston's most respected citizens, Colonel Benjamin Huger, who was still a member of the U.S. Army, convinced them not to attack. Huger even threatened to fight alongside the fort's commander, Major Robert Anderson, if the fort was attacked. The mob backed down, but it was clear to Anderson that his days at Fort Moultrie were numbered. He'd have to find another more secure place to keep his garrison—and quickly.

BENJAMIN HUGER

Benjamin Huger (1805–1877) had the military in his blood. Both of his grandfathers had served during the Revolutionary War (1775–1783), and one had been killed defending Charleston from the British. Huger graduated from the military academy at West Point and served courageously in the Mexican-American War (1846–1848).

After the battle of Fort Sumter, he reluctantly resigned from the U.S. Army and joined the Confederate cause where he served throughout the war and was promoted to major general.

After the war Huger became a farmer and lived in North Carolina and then Virginia. He returned to Charleston and died there in December 1877. The U.S. Army honored him by naming a new construction after him, "Battery Huger," which was built inside the walls of Fort Sumter. The battery was built as part of the preparations for the Spanish-American War (1898).

CHAPTER 2 A CONFEDERATE CHALLENGE

On the night of December 26, 1860, Major Anderson secretly moved his men from Fort Moultrie to Fort Sumter, which he felt offered his men better protection and was more defendable. This greatly angered the South Carolinians; however, they wasted no time in taking possession of the abandoned Fort Moultrie and manning it with troops. They also beefed up the defenses of the two other former federal forts in the harbor—Fort Johnson and Castle Pinckney—and built batteries on Morris, James, and Sullivan's Islands. In a short time, the garrison at Fort Sumter was encircled by enemy artillery—an enemy that was prepared to attack if necessary.

After Major Anderson and his federal troops left Fort Moultrie, South Carolina's troops quickly took it over.

As the weeks passed, one by one the states of the Lower South joined South Carolina in secession. Mississippi seceded on January 9, 1861, and Florida on January 10. Georgia left the Union on January 19, Louisiana on January 26, and Texas on February 1. On February 4 the seven states met to form the Confederate States of America. They named Jefferson Davis their first president and Alexander Stephens as vice president. The Confederate capital was established at Montgomery, Alabama. It moved to Richmond, Virginia, in May 1861, after that state joined the Confederacy.

THE FIGHT OVER FORT SUMTER

President Davis sent three men from Montgomery to Washington, D.C., to negotiate the evacuation of Fort Sumter. Calling the Confederacy an outlaw state, Lincoln refused to see

Fort Sumter is located on a man-made island in Charleston Harbor.

them. Lincoln was uncertain about what to do with Fort Sumter, but members of his Cabinet, including Secretary of State William Seward, believed the fort should be given over to the Confederates to avoid war. Seward also felt this was the only way to keep the remaining southern states in the Union.

U.S. Supreme Court Justice John A. Campbell of Alabama, who assisted in the negotiations, visited Seward on March 15. Seward assured him that the fort would be turned over to the Confederacy soon. But, at the time, Lincoln was not prepared to do so and was seriously considering sending much needed supplies to Anderson before he was forced to surrender Fort Sumter.

When the evacuation didn't happen, Campbell returned to Seward for answers. Seward was less confident of the future and told Campbell that supplies would not be sent to Fort Sumter "without giving notice to Governor [Francis] Pickens [of South Carolina]." Losing hope of a settlement, Campbell sent word to Jefferson Davis in Montgomery that he believed Lincoln was leaning toward war with the Confederacy.

But Lincoln was determined that if war was to come, the South would have to start it. On April 6 he gave his approval for the

steamship *Baltic* to travel to Charleston Harbor to deliver supplies to Anderson and his men at Fort Sumter. Two days later, Governor Pickens received a message from Lincoln that said if he allowed the supplies to get to Fort Sumter, the president would not send men and weapons.

Pickens promptly forwarded the message to Davis. The decision whether or not to go to war over Fort Sumter was now in Davis' hands.

Jefferson Davis

FRANCIS PICKENS

South Carolina Governor Francis Pickens (1805—1869) played a key role in the outbreak of the Civil War. A firm secessionist, he was elected governor in late 1860. It was Pickens who approved the firing on Fort Sumter's relief steamship, *Star of the West,* and later on the fort itself.

But after the Confederacy lost the war, it was also Pickens who encouraged South Carolina to rejoin the Union. "It doesn't become South Carolina to vapor or swell or strut or brag or bluster or threat or swagger," he declared. "She bids us bind up her wounds and pour on the oil of peace."

CHAPTER 3
ON THE BRINK OF WAR

Nearly everyone in President Davis' Cabinet advised him to attack Fort Sumter. However, Secretary of State Robert Toombs expressed a different point of view. "The firing on that fort will inaugurate [start] a civil war greater than any the world has yet seen . . ." he told Davis. "It puts us in the wrong. It is fatal."

But Davis would not allow the garrison to stand. He laid the blame for whatever would follow on Lincoln for not removing federal troops from Confederate territory.

He ordered General P.G.T. Beauregard, commander of Charleston Harbor, to "demand its [Sumter's] evacuation, and, if this is refused, proceed in such manner as you may determine to reduce it."

Around noon on April 11, Beauregard sent two messengers in a rowboat to the fort to deliver the message. The conditions were simple. If Anderson and his men left the fort, they would be allowed to take their personal property and be free to return to the north by ship. Anderson, having no orders to abandon the fort, refused to do so. Yet, not knowing when the supply ship would arrive, he did leave the door open for a possible surrender. "Gentlemen," he told the messengers, "if you do not batter us to pieces, we should be starved out in a few days." The men relayed this back to Beauregard, who felt that Anderson might give up without a fight if they waited long enough.

But time was running out. In the early hours of April 12, Confederate boats spotted the supply ship *Baltic* and its escort approaching the harbor. Beauregard sent four more men to the fort to give Anderson a final ultimatum. When he refused to give up the fort, he was told that Confederate guns would begin firing in one hour. The men returned to the mainland to give the order to fire on Fort Sumter.

P.G.T. BEAUREGARD

Few Confederate military leaders were as colorful or as outspoken as General Pierre Gustave Toutant Beauregard (1818–1893), who had numerous nicknames including "the Hero of Fort Sumter." He was born near New Orleans, Louisiana, and like many fellow Army officers of his generation, he saw action in the Mexican-American War.

When South Carolina seceded, Beauregard resigned his post as superintendent at West Point to become a brigadier general in the Confederate Army. After the Battle of Fort Sumter, he commanded troops at the Battles of Bull Run and Shiloh, among others. However, Beauregard didn't get along well with Jefferson Davis,

his commander in chief. Davis relieved Beauregard of his command in 1863 and sent him back to Charleston to defend the South Carolina coast.

Near the war's end, Beauregard fought in the siege of Richmond. After the South lost the war, he brought his leadership skills to the railroad, where he served as a director. Beauregard died in 1893 at age 74.

CHAPTER 4
A SOUTHERN VICTORY

The cannons at Fort Johnson were readied for firing. Roger

Pryor of Virginia, one of the four negotiators who last spoke with

Anderson, was offered the honor of firing the first shot. Knowing

the horrors that would follow, he refused, saying, "I could not

fire the first gun of the war." Another Virginian, 67-year-old

Edmund Ruffin, a newspaper editor and hardline secessionist, had

no such misgivings. He gladly accepted the honor, and at precisely

4:30 a.m. on April 12, he fired a cannon.

Edmund Ruffin fired the first shot of the Civil War.

The blast lit up the dark sky and arced its way toward Fort
Sumter. The big guns set up all across the harbor boomed in
response. The bombardment of the fort was under way with shots
fired every two minutes. Beauregard timed it that way to conserve
ammunition over what he thought might be a long siege.

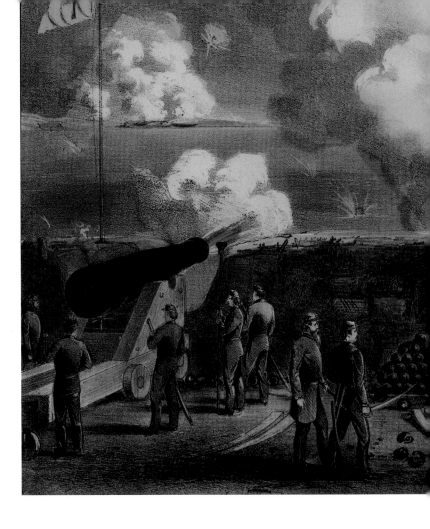

The citizens of Charleston watched the spectacle throughout the day from rooftops across the city. They cheered as the Confederate shells hit their mark. People from miles around came to Charleston by train, on horseback, and on foot to witness the siege. Among the local spectators was Mary Chesnut, the wife of former U.S. Senator James Chesnut, who was one of the last negotiators to speak to Anderson. "[T]he sound of those [Confederate] guns makes regular meals impossible," Chesnut wrote in her diary. "None of us go to [the] table. Tea-trays pervade [spread across]

The Confederates bombarded Fort Sumter (top right) from several sides.

the corridors going everywhere. Some of the anxious hearts lie on their beds and moan in solitary misery. Mrs. Wigfall and I [comfort] ourselves with tea in my room."

SURROUNDING FORT SUMTER

To bombard the fort, the Confederates used 43 guns and mortars situated at Forts Moultrie and Johnson, Cummings Point, and the floating battery. The floating battery, one of the most effective units, was a mobile battery made of pine timber

the Confederate floating battery

and palmetto logs covered with layers of railroad iron. One hundred feet (30.5 m) long, the floating battery resembled a wooden shed with four cannons mounted inside. It sat on the water and fired a total of 490 shots during the siege, delivering many devastating blows to Fort Sumter.

As the hours passed, the Confederate soldiers came to admire and respect the Union soldiers who refused to surrender despite the constant gunfire and gradual destruction of their fort. They even cheered and clapped when the quiet fort came to life with gunfire and cursed and criticized the supply ships that sat nearby for not coming to the aid of those inside the Fort Sumter garrison.

THE FLOATING BATTERY

One of the earliest known floating batteries was built and used during the French Revolution (1789–1799). It fell into disuse later but was successfully revived by French leader Napoleon III during the Crimean War (1853–1856).

The Confederate floating battery was built shortly before the Battle of Fort Sumter. On April 9, 1861, General P.G.T. Beauregard had it towed to the west end of Sullivan's Island, just a mile (1.6 km) from Fort Sumter. Although it was an effective war device, some Confederate soldiers called it the "Slaughter Pen." Many refused to serve on it, fearing they would be trapped if it was hit by Union shells.

Despite its success in the Battle of Fort Sumter, the floating battery had a short life during the Civil War. It was quickly replaced by ironclad gunboats, such as the *Merrimack* (also known as the *Virginia*). The floating battery's iron plating was dismantled to provide the covering for these Confederate boats.

But the Union men could not hold out forever, and Anderson was becoming increasingly aware of that fact. On the afternoon of April 13, when Confederate officers arrived at Fort Sumter to negotiate an evacuation, Anderson agreed to meet with them. Despite some confusion over the terms of surrender, Anderson finally agreed to abandon the fort. After 34 hours of constant bombardment, the Battle of Fort Sumter was over.

By the end of the battle, Fort Sumter was in ruins.

The news quickly reached Charleston. "They called, 'Come out—there is a crowd coming,'" Chesnut wrote in her diary. "A mob indeed, but it was headed by Colonels Chesnut and Manning. . . . They were escorted to Beauregard's headquarters. Fort Sumter had surrendered."

The next day Anderson and his men marched out of the fort and the following day headed north on the *Baltic*—the steamship that was to have brought them reinforcements and supplies. As Anderson and his men sailed out of Charleston Harbor, Confederate soldiers stood at attention along the beaches and removed their caps. It was a sign of respect for the men who were now their wartime enemies.

CHAPTER 5 THE RISE AND FALL OF A FORT

The victory at Fort Sumter was a cause for celebration throughout the Confederacy but especially in South Carolina. British journalist William Howard Russell, who visited the city three days after Sumter's fall, wrote, "Crowds of armed men singing and [dancing in] the streets . . . never was such a victory; never such brave lads; never such a fight."

The months following the Battle of Fort Sumter were strangely quiet as both the Confederates and the Union prepared for war,

Confederate troops (in gray uniforms) charged to victory over the Union Army at the Battle of Bull Run.

enlisting volunteers and outfitting them with uniforms and weapons. More than three months passed before the next major battle took place. On July 21, 1861, at Manassas, Virginia, General Beauregard, the hero of the Battle of Fort Sumter, led the Confederate troops to victory over a poorly organized Union force. The battle became known to northerners as the first Battle of Bull Run after a nearby stream. A second battle would be fought there in August of the following year.

Beauregard was called back to South Carolina in September 1862 and for very good reasons. Charleston was a strategic point that the Union wanted to seize for several reasons. First, goods and weapons from European ships were received at this main port of the South. Union warships had set up a blockade so that goods and weapons could not enter the Confederacy from abroad and cotton could not be exported. Another reason the North wanted to take Charleston was pure revenge for seizing Fort Sumter and beginning the war. Charleston was seen as the "cradle of Rebellion" and a "hornet's nest of [treason]."

Beginning in April 1863, Union Army and Navy forces assaulted the harbor and Fort Sumter, the main fort that protected it. In August, the Union Army seized Morris Island and set up big guns aimed directly at Fort Sumter. They fired nearly 45,000 shells on the fort, but could not take it. By this time, Fort Sumter was in ruins, but Beauregard would not give it up, knowing how important it was to the defense of Charleston. He moved 400 infantrymen into the fort. In July 1863 Union warships under the command of Rear Admiral John A. Dahlgren struck at Fort Sumter, but the Confederates held them back.

In the early hours of September 9, 1863, 400 Union Army and Navy volunteers approached Fort Sumter in small boats. The Confederates fired on them as they came near shore, killing or wounding about a quarter of them and taking many prisoners.

By December Union assaults on Fort Sumter had reduced it to rubble. All that was left was its earthen foundation. The explosion of an arms magazine in the fort started a fire that set off fallen shells, causing further devastation.

The Confederates finally evacuated Fort Sumter in February 1865. At 10 p.m. on February 17, Major Thomas A. Huguenin was

The Confederate flag flew above Fort Sumter during all but the last two months of the Civil War.

the last Confederate officer to leave Fort Sumter. He later wrote: ". . . I cannot describe my emotions. I felt as if every tie held dear to me was about to be severed; the pride and glory of Sumter was there, and now in the gloom of darkness we were to abandon her, for whom every one us would have shed the last drop of his blood."

Final victory for the Union came two months later when Confederate General Robert E. Lee surrendered at Appomattox Court House in Virginia. South Carolina, like much of the Confederacy, had suffered greatly in the war. Union troops under General William T. Sherman destroyed plantations and burned the capital of Columbia. It would take more than a decade for the South to fully rebuild.

Of the 63,000 soldiers from South Carolina who served in the war, about a fourth had been killed. South Carolina reentered the Union on July 9, 1868, seven and a half years after seceding.

FORT SUMTER TODAY

Today the fort where the Civil War began is a national monument that includes both Fort Sumter and Fort Moultrie. Visitors can see the reconstructed fort with several large guns in their casemates. A museum in the fort's Battery Huger contains artifacts from the Civil War era. Visitors can get a sweeping view of the harbor as the Union soldiers saw it in those tense weeks before the siege in 1861. Fort Moultrie on Sullivan's Island has a visitors' center that also features artifacts and historical exhibits.

INDEX

The Split History of the
BATTLE OF
FORT SUMTER:

UNION
PERSPECTIVE

BY STEVEN OTFINOSKI

CONTENT CONSULTANT:
Donald C. Elder III, PhD
Professor of History
Eastern New Mexico University

COMPASS POINT BOOKS
a capstone imprint

Compass Point Books are published by Capstone,
1710 Roe Crest Drive, North Mankato, Minnesota 56003
www.mycapstone.com

LIBRARY OF CONGRESS CATALOGING-IN-PUBLICATION DATA

Names: Otfinoski, Steven, author.
Title: The Split History of the Battle of Fort Sumter: A Perspectives flip book/by Steven Otfinoski.
Description: North Mankato, Minnesota: Compass Point Books, Capstone, 2018.
  Series: Perspectives Flip Books: Famous Battles | "CPB Grades 4–8."
  Includes index.
Identifiers: LCCN 2017043019 (print) | LCCN 2017043442 (ebook) |
  ISBN 9780756556891 (library binding)
  ISBN 9780756556938 (paperback)
  ISBN 9780756556976 (eBook PDF)
Subjects: LCSH: Fort Sumter (Charleston, S.C.)—Siege, 1861—Juvenile literature. | Charleston
  (S.C.)—History—Civil War, 1861–1865—Juvenile literature. | United States—History—
  Civil War, 1861–1865—Juvenile literature.
Classification: LCC E471.1 (ebook) | LCC E471.1 .O84 2018 (print) | DDC
  973.7/31—dc23

EDITOR
JENNIFER HUSTON

DESIGNER
ASHLEE SUKER

MEDIA RESEARCHER
TRACY CUMMINS

PRODUCTION SPECIALIST
KATHY MCCOLLEY

IMAGE CREDITS

Union Perspective:
Bridgeman Images: Private Collection/© Look and Learn/Bernard Platman Antiquarian Collection,
21, Virginia Historical Society, Richmond, Virginia, USA, 23, Waud, Alfred Rudolph (1828-91)
(after)/Virginia Historical Society, Richmond, Virginia, USA, 12; flickr: Internet Archive Book
Image, 27; Getty Images: Corbis Historical, 14, MPI, 16; Library of Congress Prints and Photographs
Division: 5, 7, 18, 22, Cover Bottom; Newscom: Mathew Brady Picture History, 24; North Wind
Picture Archives: Cover Top; Shutterstock: Everett Historical, 8; Wikimedia: Internet Archive Book
Images, 11, Library of Congress, 25

Confederate Perspective:
Alamy: Ivy Close Images, 12; Bridgeman Images: American Antiquarian Society, Worcester,
Massachusetts, USA, 20–21; Getty Images: Bettmann, 6, De Agostini/De Agostini Picture Library,
28, Universal History Archive, 26; Library of Congress Prints and Photographs Division: 9, 13,
22, 24, Back Cover Top; North Wind Picture Archives: Back Cover Bottom; Shutterstock: Everett
Historical, 11, Scott Alan Ritchie, 29; Wikimedia: NARA, 17, 19, Public Domain, 14, Tintazul:
Júlio Reis, 7

Printed in Canada.
010799S18

Table of Contents

CHAPTER 1

TENSION IN
CHARLESTON
HARBOR

April 1861 brought a welcoming spring to Charleston, South

Carolina. Charleston Harbor, one of the South's most beautiful

waterways, was covered with a blanket of blue sky filled with fleecy

white clouds. However, this natural beauty was at odds with the

drama that was playing out nearby. Three of the four forts that

ringed the harbor were armed with cannons and guns of all sizes in

preparation for battle. All this firepower was aimed at Fort Sumter,

the fourth and newest fort. Built of brick and stone, Fort Sumter was

perched like a jewel at the harbor's entrance. Why were the other

forts and batteries aiming their guns at Fort Sumter?

The American flag flew over Fort Sumter in the spring of 1861, but the Confederates wanted to change that.

The question could be answered by the flag that flapped in the brisk breezes above Fort Sumter—the flag of the United States. South Carolina and six other southern states were no longer a part of the United States and did not pledge their allegiance to its flag. They had formed their own nation—the Confederate States of America. Once just another federal fort, Fort Sumter was now enemy territory.

This ill will between the northern states, which represented the Union, and the southern Confederate states began long before that fateful month of April 1861. It was a conflict that had been brewing since the U.S. Constitution had been adopted in 1788. The Constitution called for a balance of power between the federal government and the governments of the individual states. But this balance was threatened by the issue of slavery.

Enslaved Africans had been brought to America since the early 1600s. By the 1700s, slavery was thriving in the South, where the agricultural economy depended on unpaid labor to support its large plantations and smaller farms. In the North, the economy was becoming more based on manufacturing and trade, so unskilled labor was less in demand and slavery gradually disappeared.

A growing number of northerners opposed slavery on moral grounds as well. Some became abolitionists who actively supported making slavery illegal in the United States. Through the first half of the 19th century, Congress debated the slavery issue. The debate grew more intense as new territories were created. Proslavery groups wanted slavery allowed in these territories, while antislavery groups wanted to stop its spread. Congress came up with a number of compromises to try to satisfy both sides. These included the policy of popular sovereignty, where the population of a new territory or state would vote to determine whether it would be a slave state or a free state. But these compromises were only temporary solutions to a more complex problem.

THE ELECTION OF ABRAHAM LINCOLN

The Republican Party was born in the 1850s. It included groups that opposed slavery and its spread. It also favored economic and political policies that benefited the North. In 1860 the Republicans nominated Abraham Lincoln, a former congressman from Illinois, as their presidential candidate. Lincoln, a Unionist who believed in a strong federal government, was a moderate on the slavery issue.

He believed slavery should not be abolished in the South, but it also shouldn't be allowed elsewhere in the country.

The Democratic Party was divided on the slavery question and split into several groups, each with its own candidate. Stephen Douglas of Illinois ran on a campaign promoting popular sovereignty. Southern Democrats nominated John C. Breckinridge of Kentucky. Breckinridge was in favor of protecting the rights of slaveholders in all new territories as well as in the South. A fourth candidate, John Bell of Tennessee, represented the Constitutional Union Party. Bell remained neutral on slavery. On Election Day, the Democratic vote was split, and Lincoln, who received only 39.8 percent of the popular vote, still won by more than 100 electoral votes.

Southerners were outraged at his election. Hatred of Lincoln and the North was particularly strong in South Carolina. Leaders of the state feared that Lincoln would take away their states' rights and end slavery, even though he had never said that.

TENSIONS MOUNT

By early December 1860, South Carolina's leaders were thinking about seceding from the Union. In preparation for that, they asked

The election of President Abraham Lincoln in 1860 angered many southerners.

President James Buchanan— who was still in office until Lincoln's inauguration in March 1861—to turn over to the state all federal property in the Charleston area. They were especially concerned about the four forts in Charleston Harbor—Fort Moultrie on Sullivan's Island, Castle Pinckney on Shutes Folly Island, Fort Johnson on James Island,

President James Buchanan

and Fort Sumter. Only a few weeks earlier, Federal Army officer Major Robert Anderson had arrived in Charleston to take command of the garrison of 85 soldiers at Fort Moultrie. Castle Pinckney and Fort Johnson were unoccupied at the time. Fort Sumter was still under construction and was only occupied by workers.

Buchanan was personally opposed to slavery, but he believed the Constitution allowed it, so he had done nothing to end it in the South. Three members of Buchanan's Cabinet who were southerners were also pressuring him to give up the forts. He refused to do so but agreed to a compromise with South Carolina. Anderson had asked the president for reinforcements at Fort Moultrie. To satisfy South Carolina's leaders, Buchanan pledged not to send the reinforcements. In return, the South Carolinians agreed not to attempt to seize Fort Moultrie while negotiations for turning over the forts were still ongoing.

But tensions continued to rise. South Carolina's leaders feared what Lincoln might do to establish federal power in their state once he was in office. The state legislature called a convention to consider the question of seceding—breaking away from the United States. On December 20, South Carolina's lawmakers voted 169–0 to secede.

In Washington Buchanan decided not to take military action against South Carolina for seceding. He wanted to give Lincoln a chance to resolve the situation in his own way. But at Fort Moultrie, Major Anderson was growing increasingly concerned. He only had a few months of supplies left. How long would it be, he wondered, before the secessionists of South Carolina would try to force him and his men out of the fort? Anderson decided he wasn't going to sit around and wait for that to happen.

FORT MOULTRIE

Fort Moultrie has a long and distinguished history. The first fort built on the site held British warships at bay in 1776 during the Revolutionary War (1775–1783) and was later named in honor of its commander, Colonel William Moultrie. The fort fell into neglect after the Revolutionary War, so in 1798, work began on a second fort on the site as part of a coastal defense system.

In 1804 a hurricane destroyed the second fort. The third and final Fort Moultrie, a five-sided masonry structure, was completed in 1809. After the Civil War, Fort Moultrie was modernized with new cannons and concrete reinforcements. It was finally decommissioned as a fort in 1947 and is now a museum and part of the Fort Sumter National Monument.

HOLDING DOWN THE FORT

*M*ajor Anderson was facing hard choices. If he remained at Fort Moultrie and the South Carolinians attacked, his troops would be extremely vulnerable. The fort was old, in poor condition, and would be difficult to defend. However, Fort Sumter, near the mouth of the harbor, was a brand-new fort made of solid granite. It would certainly offer a stronger defense. On the night of December 26, 1860, Anderson made his move. He gave his officers just 20 minutes to have their men ready to travel. Boats were engaged to transport the soldiers.

Under the cover of darkness, Major Robert Anderson moved his troops from Fort Moultrie to Fort Sumter.

A few men stayed behind at Fort Moultrie to protect the ships if the enemy's guard boats should spot them and attack. The departing soldiers took off their coats and covered their muskets so they would look like laborers returning to Fort Sumter if spotted by the guards.

The actual laborers at Fort Sumter were stunned to see the soldiers arrive. Workers who favored the South were hustled onto the boats and sent to the mainland. Those loyal to the Union remained at the fort to continue its construction.

Anderson's bold actions were condemned by the South Carolinians. They quickly occupied Fort Moultrie with their own soldiers and sent a trio of leaders to Buchanan, demanding that he give up Fort Sumter and evacuate the federal troops.

The president was urged not to do so by several of his Cabinet members. Instead, on January 5, 1861, Buchanan approved sending *Star of the West*, a merchant ship loaded with supplies and 200 soldiers, to Fort Sumter. However, he did not send word to Anderson that the ship was coming.

Star of the West arrived at Charleston Harbor on January 9. After the ship was fired upon by South Carolina's artillery, the captain turned around and went back to sea. Unsure what was happening, Anderson ordered his men not to fire at the Confederate artillery. Later, back in Washington, Buchanan refused to see the incident as an act of war because no blood was shed. He took no action against South Carolina and left it up to Lincoln to decide what to do next.

But time for a peaceful resolution was quickly running out. The same day *Star of the West* was fired upon, Mississippi joined South Carolina in secession. Five other southern states seceded

Confederate troops shot at the Star of the West *when it tried to deliver supplies to the men at Fort Sumter.*

by February 1. A week later, delegates from the seven states met in Montgomery, Alabama, and established a new nation—the Confederate States of America. They named Jefferson Davis their first president and Alexander Stephens as vice president.

By this time, nearly all the federal forts and other military installations in the Confederate states had been abandoned by their commanders. Only four forts remained in federal hands: Fort Sumter in Charleston and three forts in Florida, including Fort Pickens near Pensacola.

FORT PICKENS

The story of the federal Forts Sumter and Pickens are strikingly similar—to a point. Like Major Anderson, Lieutenant Adam Slemmer, commander of Fort Pickens, moved his men to the fort from less defensible forts in Pensacola Harbor. When troops from Florida and Alabama demanded that Slemmer surrender the fort to them, like Anderson, Slemmer refused. But that is where the similarities end.

In Florida, on January 28, 1861, the two sides agreed to a truce. The rebels would not attack the fort and the federal government would not reinforce it with more troops. Lincoln did send supplies to Fort Pickens, but the ships sat in the harbor for 10 weeks because Slemmer did not want to break the truce.

In October more than 1,000 Confederate troops landed near Fort Pickens, but they were driven back by Union troops. By the following May, the Confederates had abandoned Pensacola Harbor, and Fort Pickens stayed in Union hands for the remainder of the war.

Fort Pickens

Back in Washington, Lincoln was inaugurated on March 4, 1861. No president had ever entered office in a time of greater national crisis. In his inaugural address, the new president stated he had no intention of retaking federal facilities already held by the Confederacy. However, he clearly stated that he would "hold, occupy, and possess" those forts and other defenses still in federal control. That meant Forts Sumter and Pickens.

The next day, Lincoln arrived at his office in the White House to find a note on his desk from former Secretary of War Joseph Holt. Holt told Lincoln that Anderson had only six weeks of supplies left, and he needed help. What would Lincoln do?

LINCOLN'S DILEMMA

ith only six weeks to make a decision before Fort Sumter

would be out of supplies, Lincoln weighed his options. He could

withdraw the troops and let the Confederates have the fort. Or he

could send warships to Charleston Harbor and have them shoot

their way past the Confederate defenses in order to take supplies

and reinforcements to Fort Sumter. The first option would keep

the peace and perhaps keep the remaining states in the so-called

"Upper South" (Virginia, Tennessee, North Carolina, Kentucky,

Arkansas, and Maryland) from joining the Confederacy.

Lincoln (left) and his Cabinet

The second option would almost certainly lead to war—a war Lincoln wanted to avoid. But there was a third option. He could do nothing. In the meantime, he might find a way to resupply Fort Sumter and still avoid war. Most of Lincoln's advisers, including all but one of his Cabinet members, urged him to give up the fort. But Lincoln wasn't convinced. He felt that giving up Fort Sumter would dangerously weaken the Union and empower the Confederacy.

Most Americans agreed with Lincoln. One concerned citizen, Charles Ward, had written a letter to Buchanan on January 10, saying, "Reinforce Fort Sumter at all hazards!" By March 28, the Cabinet had reconsidered. Four of the men now supported sending supplies to Fort Sumter. One of them, Montgomery Blair, introduced the president to his brother-in-law Gustavus V. Fox, a businessman and former naval officer from Massachusetts. Fox told Lincoln his daring plan for taking

supplies to Fort Sumter. He would carry troops and supplies on a transport ship, the *Baltic*, which would be escorted by warships to Charleston Harbor. Under the cover of night, the ship would leave the men and supplies at a sandbar near the harbor. Then small boats would take the men over to Fort Sumter. The warships would stand guard and fire on any Confederates who tried to attack.

It struck Lincoln as a bold but workable plan. However, he still wanted to avoid a violent encounter, if possible. On April 6 the president sent a message to South Carolina Governor Francis Pickens saying that if the state's government allowed the *Baltic* to deliver supplies to Fort Sumter then Union troops would not fire upon the Confederates unless the Confederates fired first.

AN ULTIMATUM

Pickens forwarded the message to Davis who was angered by Lincoln's actions. He ordered General P.G.T. Beauregard to seize the fort before the transport ship arrived. In response, Beauregard demanded that Anderson and his troops evacuate the fort. Anderson refused, despite the fact that he had only a few days of supplies left. Beauregard gave him a choice: State when he would evacuate Fort Sumter, or the Confederates would begin shooting. Anderson refused, saying, "my sense of honor and my obligation to my government will prevent my compliance."

Just after midnight on the morning of April 12, Beauregard sent Colonel James Chesnut and three other men to offer Anderson a final ultimatum. The discussions lasted for several hours,

but Anderson tried to stall for more time. He told them he would evacuate in three days unless he received contrary orders from Washington or received additional supplies. Beauregard's men rejected this idea. They told him that he had one hour to get his troops off the island before the Confederate soldiers would open fire on the fort. It was 3:20 a.m. Anderson showed no fear but shook each man's hand, saying, "If we do not meet again in this world, I hope we may meet in the better one." The negotiators left, and Anderson and his men prepared for the coming battle.

MAJOR ROBERT ANDERSON

Robert Anderson (1805–1871) was not a typical Union officer. He hailed from Kentucky, a slave state, was a former slaveholder, and was sympathetic to the South's cause. But he was also a loyal federal soldier with a strong sense of duty. Earlier in his military career, Anderson had taught at the U.S. Military Academy at West Point, New York.

One of his favorite students there was P.G.T. Beauregard, who became his assistant after graduating. But Beauregard later joined the Confederacy, and in April 1861, he was preparing to attack his former teacher and his men.

CHAPTER 4
UNDER SIEGE

The first shot fired on Fort Sumter came as promised at 4:30 a.m. on April 12, 1861. It was fired from a battery situated on Cummings Point, on the mainland, only about a mile (1.6 kilometers) away. Captain Abner Doubleday, Anderson's second-in-command, found himself in the line of fire.

Doubleday later recalled, "A ball from Cummings Point lodged in the magazine wall, and by the sound seemed to bury itself in the masonry about a foot [30 centimeters] from my head, in very unpleasant proximity [nearness] to my right ear."

Confederate fire from 19 batteries grew heavy and constant, breaking off pieces of masonry in the fort, some of which fell on soldiers and injured them. To save their limited ammunition, Anderson ordered his men not to return fire.

Meanwhile, Fox and his relief ship had entered the harbor several hours earlier. He sat and waited for the warships to arrive. When the Confederates fired at the *Baltic,* Fox retreated. Later, one warship arrived on the scene. The other warship had gone to Fort Pickens instead. Fox delayed moving again until morning.

ANDERSON'S TROOPS FIGHT BACK

At 7 a.m. Anderson gave the order to return fire. There were three levels in the fort where the gunners could fire their cannons. Anderson decided that the higher levels were unsafe because the men would be too exposed to enemy fire. For their own safety, he had the gunners fire only from the lowest level. But it was so low to the ground that the shells couldn't arc high enough into the air to reach the Confederates.

All that day the bombardment continued. Fox's small fleet encountered choppy seas, and the small boats could not land safely at the fort. Fox decided to wait again until darkness fell. By then, Confederate cannons and gunfire had destroyed much of the upper part of the fort. Anderson feared the Confederates would launch an attack by storming the fort, but they only fired from their stations.

The shelling continued into the next morning. By 10 a.m. fires were spreading throughout the fort from cannonballs that

*The Civil War began when Confederate troops at Fort Moultrie
fired upon federal soldiers at Fort Sumter.*

the Confederates had heated in furnaces until they were red hot.
Anderson feared a shell would hit the main ammunition magazine
and the 300 barrels of gunpowder inside would be set on fire and
explode. He ordered soldiers to roll the barrels out of the magazine
to less vulnerable spots in the fort and cover them with wet
blankets. Meanwhile, officers chopped down all the woodwork
near the magazine to further prevent the fires from spreading.

After moving out just 96 barrels of gunpowder, Anderson
commanded the soldiers to throw the remaining barrels into the
harbor. But the tide kept sweeping the barrels back toward the
fort. Some were even set on fire by incoming Confederate shells.

After hours of constant bombardment, Fort Sumter was on fire and the brand-new fort had taken a beating.

Anderson then ordered the soldiers to close the huge copper door of the magazine to protect the barrels that had yet to be removed. But an enemy shot struck the door's lock and bent it so badly that it couldn't be reopened. This left Anderson's men unable to access the ammunition inside.

By 11 a.m. fire had eaten away about a fifth of the fort. To escape the choking smoke, some soldiers lay down on the ground and covered their mouths with handkerchiefs. Others fled to the wall openings from where the cannons were fired. There, they had a better chance of breathing fresh air.

At 12:48 p.m. the fort's flag fell when the end of the flagpole was shot down. Soldier Peter Hart fashioned a new flagpole, nailed the flag to it, and raised it again. But it was clear to Anderson that they couldn't stand the siege much longer. Ammunition was low, the men were hungry and tired, and the fires were spreading across the fort. "[A]t last," Doubleday later recalled, "nothing was left of the building but the blackened walls and smoldering embers." But miraculously, not one man had been killed or seriously wounded during the battle.

Peter Hart risked his life to raise the American flag over Fort Sumter.

THE SURRENDER OF FORT SUMTER

When the flag went down, some Confederates thought it was a sign of surrender. One of them was Colonel Louis Wigfall. In the early afternoon, Wigfall took a small rowboat— without consulting with his commander—and headed to Fort Sumter. He waved a white handkerchief from his sword to show that he came in peace. Anderson agreed to listen to his terms. Wigfall avoided using the word *surrender* but instead said

Confederate Colonel Louis Wigfall took matters into his own hands and got Major Anderson to surrender Fort Sumter.

that Anderson and his men would have to evacuate the fort. If they did so, Wigfall said, they would be allowed to take their arms and whatever baggage they could carry with them. Everything else, including all heavy artillery, would stay in the fort. Anderson agreed to the terms.

A second boat arrived soon after with officers and aides of General Beauregard. They were surprised to hear that Wigfall had already been there. Anderson was furious when he learned that the terms he had agreed to would not be honored. He was about to send the men away and resume the battle, but then another boat of Confederate officers arrived and agreed to offer the same terms that Wigfall had. They discussed with Anderson the final details of the evacuation that would take place the following morning.

The siege of Fort Sumter had lasted 34 hours with 4,000 shots and shells fired upon the structure. Anderson was told that if he had not surrendered when he did, the Confederates were prepared to storm the fort that night.

ABNER DOUBLEDAY

For all his achievements as an officer in the Civil War, Abner Doubleday (1819–1893) is best known for something with which he likely had nothing to do. After the Battle of Fort Sumter, Doubleday continued to serve in the war. He was promoted to brigadier general in February 1862 and participated in several battles, including Antietam and Gettysburg—two of the deadliest conflicts of the war.

After the war Doubleday remained in the U.S. Army and was stationed in California and Texas, where he commanded a unit of all-black soldiers. For many years it was believed that in 1839, while a student in Cooperstown, New York, Doubleday invented the modern game of baseball. More recently, this has been proven false. Doubleday actually had little interest in athletics and was a scholarly man who enjoyed a good book. Even so, the Baseball Hall of Fame is located in Cooperstown.

CHAPTER 5
FROM BATTLE TO WAR

The Union troops at Fort Sumter rose early on the morning of April 14 to make preparations to leave the fort. Fox and his fleet learned of the surrender and waited to take the evacuating soldiers back north.

Anderson insisted on leaving the fort with dignity, and when the time came, he gave the order to fire a 100-gun salute to the Union flag that would soon be lowered. No one saw the pile of live cartridges hidden under the muzzle of one of the cannons to be fired.

The first death in the Civil War came as an accident when a pile of cartridges exploded during a 100-gun salute to the American flag.

A spark from the muzzle landed on the cartridges, exploding them. The explosion blew off the right arm of gunner Daniel Hough. Five other members of the gun crew were thrown into the air. Hough died shortly after and was buried in the fort's parade ground. He was the first man killed during the Civil War.

Edward Galloway and George Fielding, two of the other five injured, were sent to a hospital in Charleston. Galloway died of his wounds a few days later, but Fielding recovered. The other injured soldiers were well enough to march from the fort with the others. They all spent the night on a Confederate steamer and were transported the next morning to the *Baltic*, which carried them to New York City.

The Confederate attack and seizure of Fort Sumter was seen in the North as an act of war. President Lincoln called for 75,000 volunteer militiamen to enter active service for 90 days to put down what he called a Confederate rebellion. He had no trouble raising the volunteers. In fact, many more volunteers from across the North were eager to fight and avenge Fort Sumter.

The Battle of Fort Sumter united the Union, bringing Republicans and many Northern Democrats together in a common cause. They could see clearly that war was the only way to defeat the Confederacy and save the Union from ruin. While the Civil War would be a long and bitter struggle lasting four years, it would finally settle the issue of whether America would truly be a united or a divided country. As Jane Stuart Woolsey of New York City wrote on May 10, 1861, the "time before Sumter" was a very different time from the time after the attack. "It seems as if we never were alive till now; never had a country till now."

THE FATE OF A SOLDIER AND HIS PRESIDENT

Robert Anderson arrived in New York City a national hero. Among his admirers was Lincoln's 8-year-old son Tad. On May 15, 1861, Lincoln promoted Anderson to brigadier general and later made him commander of the Department of Kentucky. But the strain of the siege and his old war wounds left Anderson in poor health, and he retired from active service in October 1863.

On April 9, 1865, General Robert E. Lee surrendered to Union General Ulysses S. Grant and effectively ended the Civil War. Five days later Anderson returned to Fort Sumter. In a symbolic gesture, he raised the same scorched American flag he had taken down exactly four years earlier. At a military ball in Charleston that evening, Anderson raised a toast to his president, "the good, the great and honest man, Abraham Lincoln." That same night, Lincoln was shot by assassin John Wilkes Booth and died the following morning.

Anderson retired to France in 1869 and died there on October 26, 1871. The French gave him a full military funeral before his body was sent back to the United States for burial.

INDEX

GLOSSARY

ABOLITIONIST—a person who supported the banning of slavery

BATTERY—a group of heavy guns that are all used together

BLOCKADE—a closing off of an area to keep people or supplies from going in or out

CASEMATE—a chamber in a fort with openings through which guns may be fired

DECOMMISSION—to take out of active service

GARRISON—a group of soldiers based at a fort and ready to defend it

MAGAZINE—a room or building in a fort where ammunition and explosives are stored

MILITIAMEN—a group of volunteer citizens who serve as soldiers in emergencies

MUZZLE—the opening end of a gun barrel where bullets come out

NEGOTIATIONS—discussions in order to come to an agreement

NEUTRAL—not taking any side in an argument

POPULAR SOVEREIGNTY—a policy considered before the Civil War, whereby citizens of new territories of the United States would vote to decide whether they would allow slavery

REINFORCEMENTS—an additional supply of soldiers or weapons

SECESSIONIST—a person in favor of breaking away from the United States right before the Civil War

INTERNET SITES

Use FactHound to find Internet sites related to this book.

Visit *www.facthound.com*

Just type in *9780756556891* and go.

TIMELINE

1860

November 6: Republican Abraham Lincoln is elected president

November 15: Major Robert Anderson receives orders to take command of the soldiers stationed at Fort Moultrie in Charleston Harbor

December 8: South Carolina's leaders ask President James Buchanan to turn over to the state all federal property in the Charleston area

December 20: South Carolina secedes from the Union

December 26: During the night, Major Anderson moves his troops to Fort Sumter

1861

January 5: President Buchanan approves sending the *Star of the West* to Fort Sumter

March 4: Abraham Lincoln is inaugurated president of the United States

March 5: President Lincoln receives word that the troops at Fort Sumter have only enough food and supplies to last six weeks

April 6: Lincoln approves sending the steamship *Baltic* to deliver supplies to Fort Sumter

April 11, 12:00 p.m.: General P.G.T. Beauregard sends two messengers to Fort Sumter to give Anderson a choice: Leave the fort or the Confederates will start shooting; Anderson refuses

April 12, 12:00 a.m.: Four negotiators row out to Fort Sumter to speak with Anderson; after several hours of discussion, Anderson once again refuses to evacuate

April 12, 3:20 a.m.: The Confederate negotiators tell Anderson they will begin firing in one hour

January 9: *Star of the West* arrives at Charleston Harbor but turns around when fired upon; Mississippi secedes from the Union

January 10: Florida secedes from the Union

January 11: Alabama secedes from the Union

January 19: Georgia secedes from the Union

January 26: Louisiana secedes from the Union

January 29: Kansas is admitted to the Union as a free state, meaning slavery is not allowed

February 1: Texas secedes from the Union

February 4: The seven states that have seceded from the Union meet to form the Confederate States of America

February 9: Jefferson Davis is named president of the Confederate States of America

April 12, 4:30 a.m.: The first shot of the Civil War is fired upon Fort Sumter

April 12, 7:00 a.m.: Anderson orders his men to return fire

April 13, 11:00 a.m.: After more than 18 hours of constant bombardment from the Confederates, about 20 percent of Fort Sumter has been destroyed

April 13, 12:48 p.m.: The American flag hanging at Fort Sumter falls when the flagpole is shot down; soldier Peter Hart makes a new flagpole and raises the flag once again

April 13, early afternoon: Anderson agrees to surrender following several rounds of negotiations with Confederate Colonel Louis Wigfall, aides sent by General Beauregard, and other confederate officers; after 34 hours the siege of Fort Sumter is over

April 14, around 2:00 p.m.: Daniel Hough becomes the first man killed during the Civil War when an explosion occurs during a flag ceremony just prior to the fort's evacuation

SELECT BIBLIOGRAPHY

Catton, Bruce. *The American Heritage New History of the Civil War.* New York: Viking Penguin, 1996.

Foote, Shelby. *The Civil War: A Narrative, Vol. 1 Fort Sumter to Perryville.* New York: Vintage Books, 1986.

McPherson, James. *Battle Cry of Freedom: The Civil War Era.* New York: Oxford University Press, 1988.

Simpson, Brooks D. et al, eds. *The Civil War: The First Year Told by Those Who Lived It.* New York: Penguin, 2011.

Turner, Thomas R. *101 Things You Didn't Know About the Civil War.* Avon, Mass.: Adams Media, 2000.

Wertz, Jay, and Edwin C. Bearss. *Smithsonian's Great Battles & Battlefields of the Civil War.* New York: William Morrow, 1977.

Woodhead, Henry, ed. *Charleston.* Alexandria, Va.: Time-Life Books, 1997.

FURTHER READING

Cummings, Judy Dodge. *The Civil War: The Struggle that Divided America.* White River Junction, Vt.: Nomad Press, 2017.

George, Enzo. *The Civil War.* New York: Cavendish Square Publishing, 2015.

Mattern, Joanne. *Fort Sumter.* Vero Beach, Fla.: Rourke Publishing Group, 2015.

Samuels, Charlie. *The Attack on Fort Sumter.* New York: Gareth Stevens Publishing, 2014.

CRITICAL THINKING QUESTIONS

1. Why was Fort Sumter so important to the Union before the outbreak of the Civil War? And why was the fort and the city of Charleston and its harbor such an important target for the Union during the war after it fell into Confederate hands? Use evidence from the text to support your answers.

2. President Abraham Lincoln faced a difficult decision when he sent supplies and reinforcements to Fort Sumter. Do you think he made the right decision? Why or why not? Refer to the text in your answer.

3. Major Robert Anderson and General P.G.T. Beauregard were both U.S. military officers before the war and both were southerners. Why do you think they ended up on opposite sides? What factors influenced their decisions? Refer to the text and possible outside sources to support your answer.